KT-416-182 ✔

...can be dangerous. ...break bones, ...ok explains ...a training manual. If you plan to ...sing the right equipment, and choosing ...that you're ready for.

A WORD ABOUT HELMETS AND PADS: Some of the boarders pictured in this book are not wearing helmets, knee and elbow pads, or other protective equipment. This is a dangerous choice. You should wear a helmet and pads whenever you get on a skateboard. It's your body—take care of it.

If you do go out and break your head or any other part of your body or anyone else's body, don't blame National Geographic. We told you to be careful!

(Translation into legalese: Neither the publisher nor the author shall be liable for any bodily harm that may be caused or sustained as a result of conducting any of the activities described in this book.)

One of the world's largest nonprofit scientific and educational organizations, the National Geographic Society was founded in 1888 "for the increase and diffusion of geographic knowledge." Fulfilling this mission, the Society educates and inspires millions every day through its magazines, books, television programs, videos, maps and atlases, research grants, the National Geographic Bee, teacher workshops, and innovative classroom materials. The Society is supported through membership dues, charitable gifts, and income from the sale of its educational products. This support is vital to National Geographic's mission to increase global understanding and promote conservation of our planet through exploration, research, and education.

For more information, please call 1-800-NGS LINE (647-5463) or write to the following address:
National Geographic Society
1145 17th Street N.W.
Washington, D.C. 20036-4688 U.S.A.
Visit the Society's Web site at www.nationalgeographic.com.

NATIONAL GEOGRAPHIC

EXTREME Sports

SKATEBOARD!

Your Guide to Street, Vert, Downhill, and More.

BY CONSTANCE LOIZOS

Illustrations Jack Dickason

NATIONAL GEOGRAPHIC

WASHINGTON, D.C.

Tony Hawk grabs his skateboard as he jumps from the ramp during the 2001 X Games in San Diego, California.

What's Inside

Let It Roll

Do you love speed, adventure, and the exhilaration that comes from being truly creative?

Explore the world of skateboarding, one of the oldest, and coolest, of extreme sports. Consider your first roller-coaster ride—the aerial twists and turns, the thrill of face-flapping speeds at which the downhills took you back to Earth. Skateboarding offers the same extremes. Even better, it lets you control your own thrills. Skateboarding is all about raw talent, athleticism, agility, nerve, and, maybe most importantly, dedication. It's also a blast.

Read on to learn how the pros race faster, skate higher, land tricks, and wind more times in midair than laundry on a clothesline. Find out what gear the street crowd uses to turn curbs into launch pads, and learn how to bomb down a hill with absolute fearlessness.

There's nothing like the triumph you'll feel from going big and pushing your limits.

Extreme Sports

Part 1

Get On Board

- **Wheel Power**
- **Board Sick**
- **First Moves**

With a bit of experience, you begin to recognize skateboarding as more than a thrill ride. Face it, skateboarding has moved beyond a simple pastime into a serious sport.

Wheel Power

You don't need a lot of equipment to get going. Just put your board on the ground, step on it, and you're on your way.

Whether you're ripping it in your backyard or in a skatepark that's nearby, skateboarding isn't limited by location. You can do it virtually anywhere. Just stay off the street where it is limited—by the law. (Skateboarding on city streets is illegal nearly everywhere.)

GETTING IT GOING

From simple beginnings in the early 1900s, when inventive kids began nailing roller-skating trucks and wheels to the bottom of a wood plank, this new adventurous activity was so fun, it couldn't help but become a phenomenon. And the momentum hasn't slowed down a bit. Skateboarding today is more popular than it's ever been.

DO IT

The biggest challenge any skateboarder faces has nothing to do with halfpipes or ramps. It's gaining confidence, and that is achieved by being smart and unremitting. Don't back down or give up. As with any endeavor, if you want to rock at this sport, you have to keep at it. Simply, practice. Work up to the hard tricks by starting with the easier ones. Before you know it, you'll be carving it up like the best of them. Just don't forget that, first and foremost, you're out to have fun.

SKATE LINGO

AIR: "To air" is to jump into the air; also called an "aerial."

BACKSIDE: When a trick is executed with your back to the ramp or obstacle.

BANK: Any obstacle that you can ride up and down (a ramp, for example).

BUST: To get a trick right, or to skate well.

CARVE: To make turns by shifting your weight back and forth.

COMPLETE: A skateboard loaded with all the necessities: deck, grip tape, wheels, trucks, and bearings (see p. 13).

COPING: The material on the edge of an obstacle where you grind and slide.

DARKSIDE: The bottom of the skateboard.

FAKIE: Skating in switch stance (see p. 15) with your dominant foot (the one that feels less natural) in front.

GRIND: To balance and often slide the trucks or bottom of the board against a curb, railing, or other surface.

HALFPIPE: U-shaped ramps of any size, with a flat spot in the middle for performing tricks. Also known as "vert (vertical) ramps."

LAND: To perform a trick correctly without falling.

LEDGE: Any obstacle where you grind and slide.

PUMP: To straighten your legs in order to build up speed while riding on a transition. Also called "gyrate."

SESSION: When a bunch of skaters gather to do tricks.

SLAM: When you fall down and it hurts.

TRANSITION: The surface in between the vertical and horizontal parts of a ramp or obstacle. Also called a "tranny."

Board
Sick

One of the coolest aspects of skateboarding is just how little is required to get going.

There are just four parts of a skateboard to consider if you aren't buying it complete, and piecing them together is almost as killer as the ride itself.

DECKS

The actual board is made of laminated wood plies. The earliest skateboarders in the 1930s and 1940s made decks themselves using old 2x4s. These worked for rolling and carving, but not much more. Today, the sizes of decks are around 7½ to 9 inches (19 to 23 centimeters) wide, 32 inches (81 cm) long, and about ½-inch (1 cm) thick.

TRUCKS

Mounted to the bottom of the board, the trucks are metal components to which the wheels are attached. The first trucks consisted of not much more than the axles of roller skates. In the mid-1960s, aluminum trucks, designed specifically for skateboarding, were produced. Aside from minor changes in shape, trucks have remained fairly consistent and are still made almost exclusively of aluminum.

WHEELS

Steel wheels are no fun. Hit an unwieldy piece of gravel and you're off your board and out of control in seconds. This largely explains why the steel roller-skate wheels of the early 1950s skateboards didn't last long.

The clay wheels that replaced them weren't much better. When urethane wheels emerged, they revolutionized skateboarding. The wheels were smoother-riding, stronger, tougher, and more durable.

BEARINGS

Bearings are placed between the axle of the truck and the wheel to allow the wheel to turn as smoothly as possible. The first precision bearings were introduced in 1974, and they have hardly changed a bit since. Bearings helped turn skateboarding into a legitimate means of transportation—and a serious sport. In fact, all any rider really needs to look for in bearings is that they are ABEC 1-rated, meaning they are top-notch.

FOOT STUFF

Since the top of a skateboard is covered in sandpaper-like grip tape, the many tricks requiring you to slide across your board will seriously abuse your shoes. Fortunately, there are shoes specially designed for skateboarding, with features that stave off wear and tear. They have double- and triple-stitching to keep the shoes together and ultra-thick rubber soles. To keep regular shoes going, you can squirt Shoe Goo onto worn-down shoe heels to rebuild them, or apply it to shoe soles to make them less slippery. It can actually be used to keep any part of the shoe from falling off.

First Moves

You know you want to get on the board. Here's what to do.

Start simple. You need to learn to crawl before you can walk, and you need to know how to stand on the board and get it going before you can do complex tricks.

This dude is riding goofy (right foot in front).

START

Some skateboarders ride "goofy." That doesn't mean they look weird or do wacky things on their skateboards. Rather, riding goofy means that when you are cruising, your right foot is in front. Riding "regular," conversely, means that your left foot is in front, with your right foot on the tail.

It doesn't matter if you are left-handed or right-handed; whichever feels more comfortable is the way you will ride. That is, unless you are riding in "switch" stance. Doing switch stance means placing the foot forward that feels less natural there—all for the sake of becoming more advanced. One way not to stand is "mongo"— pushing off with your front foot while stabilizing the board with your back foot. Doing so prevents you from setting up properly when you push off and keeps you from doing tricks quickly.

STOP

It isn't rocket science, but stopping your board isn't always a piece of cake. Do it the wrong way and you'll find yourself in a Wile E. Coyote–like predicament—in midair with nothing beneath you!

When riding slowly, the easiest way to stop is to use as a brake the foot that's at the back end of your board (the right foot in regular stance) by touching it to the ground on the right-hand side. You can also carve speed away by making wide, sharp turns that will create friction between the wheels and the ground to slow you down. Just remember not to zigzag using small turns, or you'll actually speed yourself up.

SLIDE

If you're moving fast and you want to stop, try a slide. Start by shifting your weight to one side of the board. If you're going to the left, push the back wheels forward 90 degrees in a counterclockwise direction (If right, clockwise). The board will slide sideways to the direction you're moving until you come to a stop.

Once you get more advanced, add some flair with the Coleman slide, illustrated here. First, crouch all the way down with knees together. Drop your back knee toward your front foot, pointing downhill. Wearing special skateboarding gloves with plastic guards, plunk one hand on the ground, next to your body. Swing the other hand forward, reaching in the direction of

the slide, and lean to the inside of your board; then start a turn. As the board starts to slide, lift to a place of balance. Your downhill hand should continue reaching in the direction of the slide. After sliding about 180 degrees, you'll be riding backwards. At that point, all you need to do is stay crouched and compressed.

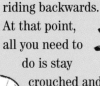

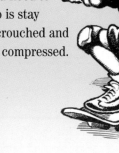

Extreme Sports

Part 2

Skate Tricky

The best part about skateboarding? It's the ultimate freedom—you choose the board you want to ride, the tricks you want to do, and the style you want to do them in.

Street Skating

There's a feeling of creativity you can only get from street skating. You make up the course from whatever obstacles are around.

S treet skating is for people too independent for more regimented sports and too intrepid to sit on the sidelines.

STREET START

The foot of San Francisco's Market Street was the birth-
place of serious street skateboarding. Street skating is,
literally, riding your board over and off sturdy public
structures like city street curbs, park benches, handrails—
even down stairs.

Until the patch of land in San Francisco now known as
Justin Herman Plaza underwent a major redevelopment in
the 1960s, the type of street skating that was being prac-
ticed was limited mostly to doing tricks in the street and
on curbs. However, after the area was built into the center
of activity it is today—with its vast plazas, handrails, and
fountains—skateboarders were too enticed by what was
being constructed to merely pass it by. They turned the
plaza into their own obstacle course, skating on, over, and
around the structures, and ultimately launched a new form
of street skateboarding.

PARK IT

Today, what was a skate laboratory for them has turned
into a hugely popular sport. Unfortunately, street skating is
illegal outside of designated areas, like skateparks, because
of the damage to public property that grinding on handrails
and curbs causes. Skating at Justin Herman Plaza is no
longer allowed.

Thankfully, plenty of skateparks and skate camps have
sprung up that have the handrails, steps, and ramps that
reflect the sport's street origins, while also giving skateboarders their own territory.

Hit the Street

Street skateboarding offers an endless variety of new tricks and maneuvers to try and to create.

Skateboarders advance and change the sport by inventing new moves. It's all part of the glory.

STREET TRICKS

OLLIE: A jump done by tapping the tail of the board on the ground with your back foot, then leaping into the air; the basis of most skating tricks.

NOLLIE: Similar to an ollie, except you kick down on the front of your board instead of the tail.

POP SHOVE-IT: An ollie in which you kick the board around 180 degrees while you're in the air, landing on it with the tail where the head was before.

KICKFLIP: Another variation of the ollie—while in the air, you kick down on the front of the board to spin it 360 degrees towards you along its axis.

HEELFLIP: Similar to a kickflip, except you kick with your heel on the front side of the board, so the spin goes in the opposite direction.

50-50 GRIND: Usually the first grinding trick a skater learns. Starting parallel to an obstacle such as a rail, curb, or ledge, ollie onto it so both trucks grind against it, then pop—or jump—off.

BOARDSLIDE: Just like a grind, but instead of being parallel to the obstacle, you're perpendicular or 90 degrees to it, so the center of the bottom of your board grinds along the edge.

THE ORIGIN OF THE OLLIE

Former pro skater Stacy Peralta first discovered someone doing an ollie in the summer of 1977, while on a skate tour with *Skateboarder* magazine. Peralta and the magazine's crew had stopped off at a skatepark in Fort Lauderdale, Florida, and an hour into his session, he was interrupted by a local kid who wanted to show Peralta a move of his own.

The kid, Alan "Ollie" Gelfand, proceeded to skate down a three-foot cement bowl at the park and, after reaching the top, suddenly popped his board off the cement lip, lifted it into midair, and switched 180 degrees to land back in the bowl with the front of the board pointing down. He told Peralta that his friends decided to call his popping maneuver the "ollie." The ollie has revolutionized both street and vert (see p. 24) skating and is now one of the most essential tricks.

Street Stunts

*Now that you can stand
on your skateboard, what's next?
Tricks. Here are a bunch of moves that
you'll have loads of fun with.*

The first tricks to try are ollies and
kickflips, the building blocks for
trick combinations. Once you've mastered
those, move on to ollie-ing off things,
like stairs or your driveway's curb.

TRY IT

OLLIE: It's all about timing. Put your back foot all
the way to the end of the tail and your front foot in the
middle. Stomp on the tail of the board with your back
foot, so it hits the ground, then immediately hop off that
foot, pushing forward with your front foot, and sliding it to

the nose. Then, level your board and drop down. Don't move your front foot back to the middle or you'll snap your board.

KICKFLIP: The kickflip is just an extension of the ollie. Just after you stomp down with your tail-end foot, kick on the heel edge of your board with the front of your other foot. Hover above your board as it spins. Then land your feet on the board in the air, letting yourself fall with it to the ground.

THE PERFECT BOARDSLIDE: Approach the rail at a moderate speed. You can roll parallel to the rail or at a slight angle if it's a bit too high. Have your feet in position to ollie. As you ollie, stick the board down onto the rail, staying directly over it with your feet evenly spread. When you get to the end, simply rotate your shoulders back around and let the board follow your weight. As you hit the ground, let the back wheels hit and pivot out of the trick.

Just remember: Even though you're itching to get out there and perfect these maneuvers, the only way to really nail them—and that means safely—is to seek out an instructor or someone who can correct you when you're doing something wrong. It'll get you up to speed five times faster than teaching yourself, and it will likely prevent you from getting injured.

VARIATIONS AND COMBINATIONS

Today, a huge number of fear-flouting tricks have been introduced by both pros and creative amateurs. One thing they all have in common is that they combine basic tricks or make them more challenging.

Frontside noseslide: A variation of the boardslide, you start this trick by riding parallel to an obstacle. Then ollie into the air and rotate 90 degrees. Instead of landing with the edge of the obstacle against the center of your board (as in a boardslide), it should be between the front trucks and the nose of the board. Balance or slide, then pop off and continue riding when you're ready.

Trey-flip (360-flip): A combination of an ollie, a kickflip, and a shove-it—to the max. To do this trick, you have to be able to ollie into the air and get a lot of hang time. You kick your front foot down as in a normal kickflip, but at the same time, do a pop shove-it with your back foot. Unlike in a normal pop shove-it, though, you need to kick the board around an entire 360 degrees. This is a tough combination!

Vert Skating

Vert skating isn't for the faint of heart.

If you have the self-motivation and discipline to keep trying what at first seems impossible, you'll be skating on ramps and halfpipes in no time at all—and loving it.

GOING VERT

Vert skating—short for vertical—is for skateboarders with an unquenchable craving for challenge and risk. Vert is second only to street skateboarding in terms of popularity. Unlike street skaters, who stay close to the ground (at least, when they aren't flying down a handrail), vert skaters are always striving for the sky, usually in bowls, ramps, and halfpipes at their local skatepark.

POOL DAYS

Vert skating started along the beaches of Los Angeles in the 1960s, when the sport was enjoying its first surge in popularity and skaters were trying to figure out new ways to maximize the fun to be had on their boards. Legend has it that the very first instance of vert skating was at the home of a skater in Southern California who drained his parents' pool while they were away on a trip so that he and his pals could roll toward the deep end. Carving higher and higher, the boarders realized that riding up the walls of the pool could unleash a whole new set of tricks, and by the end of the 1970s, during the sport's second wave of popularity, pool skating had taken off in a major way. Not only had skaters begun creating complicated aerial moves using ramps in addition to pools (which never were legal), but skateboarding contests also began to include a vert skating category.

In-Vert

*Trying to trick gravity
is no easy feat.*

Start with the basics. That means learning the essentials of ramp skating, including what kinds of wheels to use and how best to drop in on different-sized ramps.

*A silhouette of Buster
Halterman as he skates down
the ramp during the 2000
X Games in San Francisco,
California*

GETTING STARTED

The first step is to learn how to pump and ride fakie. First, get out in the middle of a small halfpipe, and push off so you go up toward one side, bending your knees and leaning into the curve. On the down slope, just let the board fall the way it went up without switching your stance. You'll be in fakie stance. Get used to the feel.

Next: pumping. Start from the bottom of the halfpipe. Push off and ride up the side, straightening your legs. When you start to descend, bend both knees and push down on the board. Ride up the other side going fakie, and do the same thing. The better you become at this maneuver, the faster and higher you'll find yourself going on the halfpipe.

THE KEY MANEUVER

After learning to pump and ride fakie, you need to know how to get into the halfpipe by "dropping in," that is, starting from a platform at the top of the halfpipe. First, keep in mind that the higher you are when dropping in, the more you'll have to bend your knees. From a height of 14 feet, you'll have to hunker down pretty tightly to stay on the board. Start on small transitions, and then work your way higher.

(1) To begin, place the tail of your board on the halfpipe's deck—the platform on which you stand before dropping in from the top—with your back wheels and trucks locked up against the coping (the strip of rubbery material on the rim of the halfpipe). Remember: You have to have confidence and commit to this fully, or you'll most likely fall. **(2)** Place your back foot on the tail and then, when you're ready, put your front foot down on the board, leaning forward at the same time. Center your weight over the front truck until your wheels hit the ramp. **(3)** Then center your weight over the middle of the board and stand up a bit. **(4)** If you aren't standing up when you reach the bottom, climb right back up there and try it again. Remember, it's only terrifying the first time.

1.

2.

3.

4.

Ramp Up

Three basic vert moves can help produce your first ramp-related bag of tricks.

Tony Hawk flips as he grabs his board as Andy MacDonald skates next to him during the X Games at Piers 30 and 32 in San Francisco, California.

FAKIE TAILSTALL

Start by dropping in on one side of a small half-pipe and riding across the pipe to the other deck. Then, ride down the other side fakie, all the while keeping your feet in the same position as they were for the drop-in.

As you approach the drop-in side, start pushing down on the tail of the board with your back foot. When you reach the coping, push the tail down more, just enough to stall there. Drop back in using your normal stance.

THE FAKIE ROCK

The fakie rock is the second big trick. To do it, ride up the other side of the ramp and press the tail down when you're near the coping so that your front wheels clear it. Next, press down on the nose a bit to lift the back wheels and "rock" on the coping with your board. Finally, press down on the tail enough to allow your wheels to clear the coping and drop back in fakie. Be careful not to press down too hard or you'll fall down backwards.

AXLE STALL

The third trick is the axle stall. Start by dropping in from one side with your knees bent slightly. When you approach the top of the other side, press down on the tail and start turning. When you feel your back truck come in contact with the coping, remain centered over your back truck and continue turning. Rock your weight on your heel and set the front truck down by shifting your weight to the center of the board. Stand up completely, rocking on your heels to stay balanced. To drop back in, center your weight over the back truck, pressing down on the tail, and lift your front truck off the coping. Turn on your back truck in towards the toe edge of your board, and turn the board into the ramp. When you're straight, set the wheels back on the ramp by pushing down with your front foot, and center your weight over the front truck. Keep your balance and roll in. This move can be done backside or frontside. Try backside first— it's easier.

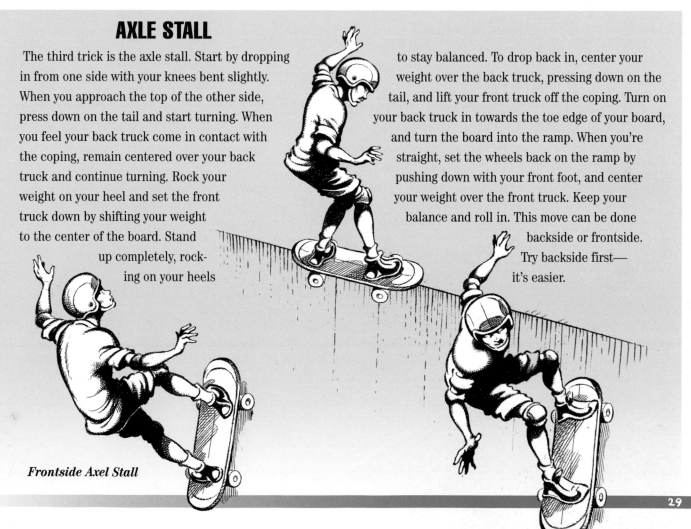

Frontside Axel Stall

Freestyle

Freestyle tricks have been a big part of skateboarding since skateboarders in the 1970s took creative skating to a whole new level.

The culture has changed some since the early days of freestyle skating, as have the skateboarders, of course. Yet freestyle tricks have only grown more wild over the last three decades.

SICK AND TWISTED

Freestyle skating is just what it sounds like. It's all about not limiting yourself to a particular style of skateboarding and doing anything you want, even if it's the funky chicken (not that we'd advise it). The moves are up to each boarder's individual style, imagination, and interpretation, which is what can make it so exciting. For example, many freestylers use their hands in a variety of ways. Sometimes, it's to do one-handed handstands. Or, it might be to perform a "finger flip," which involves flipping your board with your feet 360 degrees while you're in the middle of a handstand, then landing on the board, once its wheels hit the ground.

COMEBACK

In decades past, specifically the mid-1970s, freestyle skateboarding was all the rage. It has become less popular over the years because it became associated with the people who first launched the movement. It's viewed now as "old school" by those newer to the skate scene.

But recently, the sport has been enjoying a resurgence. The "anything goes" philosophy of freestyle makes contests a little harder to judge, but it gives skaters all of the freedom in the world to make up their own tricks—tricks whose difficulty, style, and artistry the boarder decides on his or her own.

Extreme Sports

Part 3

All Downhill

- Longboarding
- Street Luge
- Mountainboarding
- Slalom

Street luging in Los Angeles, California.

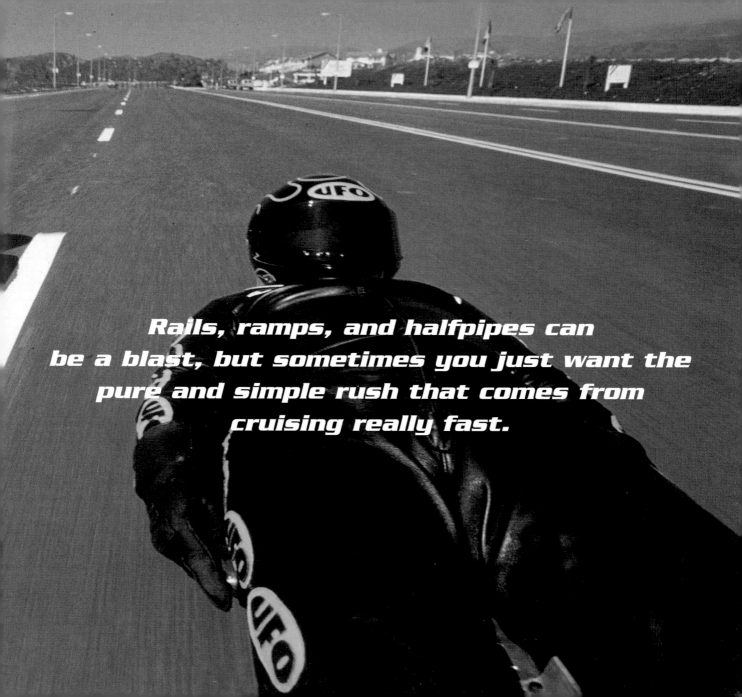

Rails, ramps, and halfpipes can
be a blast, but sometimes you just want the
pure and simple rush that comes from
cruising really fast.

Longboarding

When going somewhere is more about the ride than the destination, grabbing your longboard is an excellent transportation choice.

While regular boards are for skaters who want to master kickflips and ollies, longboards are for those with an urge to cruise, be it driveways, parking lots, or neighborhood streets.

GOING LONG

Why does adding a foot or two of length to a skate-board make the ride such an altered and compelling experience? In a word: simplicity. Longboarding isn't about flipping or grinding. It's about catching air and coasting freely. It's about jumping on and rolling.

GOING FAST

It's also about cruising fast. In fact, the world record skateboarding speed of 62 mph (100 kph) was reached on a longboard. The long wheel base on long-boards makes them more stable. The bigger, softer wheels absorb road vibrations and also lessen the speed wobble that riders experience going downhill on more traditional boards.

Unlike traditional skateboards, which are around 24 inches (61 cm) long, most longboards range in length from 36 to 72 inches (91 to 183 cm) and have loose trucks that make turning easier, sharper, and faster. Originated in the mid-1960s, the longboard's deck also has lots more flex to it, which makes the ride a quality one. (A shorter deck is usually pretty stiff and better for doing tricks. It also breaks more readily than the longboard's deck, so short boards have to be replaced more often, too.)

THE TWO MOVES

The longboard doesn't take long to master.
There are only two moves.

BOMBING

Riding straight down for maximum speed, which is, technically speaking, a piece of cake. To do it, you place your feet near the front of the board in an L shape, crouch down, slap your hands together as in prayer, then point them in front of you and push off the ground with your foot. Essentially, the idea is to make yourself more aerodynamic.

CARVING

Crisscrossing down a slope to control speed. It's usually accompanied by a hissing noise emanating from your back wheels. Don't be alarmed. They're just sliding slightly as they lose speed. Also worth noting: If you're using traditional trucks, on a decent incline, you need at least one lane of a normal-width road to carve across.

Longboards are also really great if you are a snowboarder or surfer and want to squeeze in some cross-training. BMW, for example, recently introduced a skateboard that tries to recreate the feeling of surfing, but on dry land. Called the *Streetcarver*, it has an elaborate steering system that makes carving a cinch. It even uses some of the same suspension design that the company uses in its cars.

Street Luge

Downhill was huge once, about 30 years ago, especially on the California skate scene. But with the equipment still in its earliest, imperfect days, and speeds reaching levels of 60 mph (97 kph) or greater, it came to be viewed as dangerous, and the sport went underground.

Today, downhilling has reemerged in a major way, and it's called street luge. For some idea of what street luge is like, imagine yourself whizzing downhill on a country road, through twists and turns, at bracing speeds—all while you're lying flat on your back with your head less than an inch from the pavement. It sounds crazy, and it is, sort of. It's also gaining ground—and fans—with each passing season.

Michael Colabella rolls down the hill during the street luge dual competition during the 2001 X Games in San Diego, California.

LUGE YOUR COOL

Here's how the sport works: A street luger lies flat on his or her back and depends on subtle shifts of the body to maintain control. Each sled has to be built to fit the competitor.

Because street luge is more dangerous than run-of-the-mill skateboarding, the gear required is more extensive. Along with the essentials—including the board, which looks a lot like a slim, overgrown skateboard—street-luge pilots typically wear leather full-body suits for protection, along with full-faced motorcycle helmets. They also wear leather gloves and rubber-soled shoes to protect their hands and feet.

The shoes actually perform a second function as the brakes of the street luge. The pilot plants both feet on the ground and applies pressure to slow down or stop, which is no easy maneuver. You can quickly get caught up in some major speed.

COME TOGETHER

While the exact origin of street luge differs depending on whom you ask—most pros say it started in Los Angeles years ago—it's safe to say that the idea was born when the first gutsy skateboarder dropped his board to the pavement and pointed his feet downhill. The equipment has evolved a lot since those days.

Today, riders don't typically street luge alone, especially during competition. Instead, there are four-person and six-person teams, with the groups sometimes slamming into one another at the base of whatever they are descending. (Think demolition derby!)

Michael "Biker" Sherlock makes the turn in the Street Luge Event during the 2001 X Games in San Diego, California.

Mountainboarding

Most boarders skate on flat land or down hills. These guys roll down mountains.

Once upon a time, two guys were lamenting the end of ski season when they reasoned that there had to be a way to carve down a mountain all year long. What they envisioned were slope-shredding, rock-hopping mountainboards, the first of which were brought to life in the early 1990s.

DOWNHILL FROM HERE

As close to snowboards as to skateboards, most mountainboards have flexible decks, shock suspension, bindings that let feet slide out easily, and four pneumatic tires that usually range in diameter from 9 to 12 inches (23 to 30 cm)—big enough, in other words, to roll over small obstacles. As in snowboarding, turning on a mountainboard requires that riders alternate pressure from the heels to toes. And on intense curves, a mountainboarder skims a hand over the ground for stability. Boarders wear a basic sneaker with good tread.

THE UPSIDE

You can catch big air, take six-foot drops, and even do tricks while bombing down hills, logging roads, and uncrowded hiking trails. (As with skateboarding, riding your mountainboard on city streets is illegal. Of course, street riding would kind of defeat the purpose anyway.)

THE DOWNSIDE

Wiping out can mean crashing head first into hard-packed dirt, pointy rocks, and tree stumps, all of which cause a lot more damage than anything you'll come across on a skateboard. It's also a lot harder to slow down or stop on a mountainboard. Some boards have cantilever brakes, like mountain bikes. Others use drum brakes. But most have no brakes at all. Riders skid to a stop or, more often, just hit the ground, which is why most riders are urged to wear helmets and heavy-duty padding. Riders

cover their knees, guard their wrists, wear thick leather gloves, sturdy helmets, goggles—even butt pads. And mountainboards aren't cheap. Basic models cost $150, but more deluxe versions are upwards of $400.

WHERE TO GO

The best places to mountainboard are ski areas, mountainbiking trails, skateparks, and BMX biking tracks.

Slalom

A slalom skater weaves around a row of cones, leading the board with each strong twist of waist, arms, and body, just as in skiing.

Slalom skateboarding has its roots in slalom skiing, where skiers zip around gates placed along a steep downhill course.

GO EURO

As with freestyle skating, slalom enjoyed its period of greatest popularity back in the 1970s, when many races were organized around it. Today, most slalom competitions take place in Europe, especially Switzerland, where the sport has picked up a lot of fans. In the United States, it's harder to come across an event, but you can find them if you do a little investigating. In fact, an increasing number of companies are beginning to make slalom decks (which are slightly longer than regular decks) again, which may lead to a resurgence in slalom as a competitive event. In the meantime, it can be a fun add-on to your skateboarding bag of tricks.

CONE-HEADS

There are three types of slalom: (1) Giant slalom—typically against a clock—with cones placed farther apart than in other forms of slalom races; (2) Tight slalom, in which competitors either race head-to-head, or against the clock (the cones in these races are placed close); and (3) Banked slalom, which happens at skateparks in long runs that look like concrete ditches. The boarders weave through the cones by riding up and down the banks of the runs.

CARVING

In slalom, carving is used to turn on a flat plane and to weave around the cones. You need to balance your weight at the front of the board, which causes it to flex toward the ground. When you then lean in the other direction, the board will typically jump slightly, flexing back into its normal position so another turn can be carved.

Competing

- Step Up
- Judge-Mental
- The Games

A birds-eye view of the skateboarding bowl at Mervin's California Beach Bash 2000 in Hermosa Beach, California.

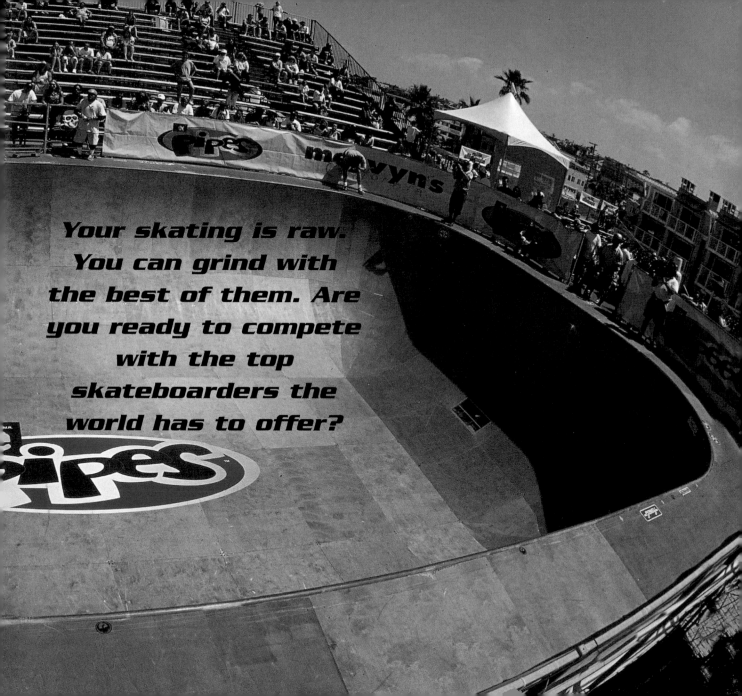

Your skating is raw. You can grind with the best of them. Are you ready to compete with the top skateboarders the world has to offer?

Step Up

Twenty years ago, skateboarding was as far from a spectator sport as California is from Caracas. But with the new interest in extreme sports and the X Games, competitions are now packed with thousands of fans.

At a skateboard competition, watching people who have perfected the craft can be mind-blowing. They can also prove to be must-see events for boarders looking for new ideas and ways to improve and perfect their tricks.

Andy McDonald juggles his board during the men's skateboard vert competition at the 2001 X Games in Philadelphia, Pennsylvania.

WATCH AND LEARN

If you aren't a pro (yet), and you plan on showing up to watch some athletes who are, you'll quickly note that most skateboarding competitions fall into one of two categories: street and vert. Street luge is also gaining in popularity, and you'll occasionally see a freestyle or slalom event.

WHY COMPETE?

It's simple: money. What better way to earn a living than by doing what you love? Generally, prize money in skateboarding is considered small potatoes when compared with many professional sports (although it's hardly chump change). Instead, the big money in this sport is tied into endorsements and merchandising. Top skaters are paid to wear shoes, shirts, sunglasses, and hats. The boards, too, have as many advertising decals as a drag-racing car.

STREET

Street competitions are usually comprised of man-made courses of rails, miniramps, banks, and other obstacles meant to duplicate the steps, curbs, hills, and benches that skaters use to test themselves day-to-day. These aren't obstacle courses, and there are usually no finish lines. Skaters can attempt whatever they want.

VERT

In vert competitions, you'll usually see the skaters grinding on ramps, particularly halfpipes, and boxes. Boxes are massive plywood boxes that usually have both sloping and sharp angles. Vert tricks are the most stunning tricks to see and do, with skaters sometimes soaring ten feet above the lip of the pipe. But flying highest doesn't automatically translate into a win, and a fall doesn't mean disqualification.

STREET LUGE COMPETITION

There are now officially-sanctioned annual events throughout Europe, Australia, and the United States, almost all of which involve four- or six-person groups. In four-person contests, four competitors push out of the starting gate and race down the course. The first luger to cross the finish line in control of the sled wins the heat. Six lugers begin each race in the six-person competition, but they rarely all cross the finish line. Navigating tight turns as they charge downhill, the racers struggle to keep their sleds upright. The first competitor to cross the finish line wins.

Judge-Mental

Skateboarding competitions can be a lot of fun for the participants, but the judging (and the prizes) are no joke.

n both the street and vert competitions, skaters have a set amount of time on the course—usually 45 seconds to a minute. Unlike sports such as figure skating, in skateboard competitions there are no compulsories.

The skateboard PARK competition for the 2001 X Games at the First Union Center in Philadelphia, Pennsylvania.

SCORING

Scores from 0 to 100 are assigned by a panel of five to six judges, with the highest and lowest marks tossed out. The remainder is then averaged, and the skateboarder with the highest score wins.

WHAT THEY'RE WATCHING

1. Style
2. The difficulty of tricks attempted
3. The flow of the skater's entire run

THE PURSE

At the X Games, money is a key incentive. In fact, it can be a cash bonanza for some of the best athletes. In 2001, the X Games' total purse was $1 million. The athletes finishing in the top three of each event see the biggest coin. Park and vert skateboarders make the most, earning $20,000 for a gold medal, $11,000 for a silver medal, and $8,000 for a bronze medal. Street lugers make the least. First place will win the top contestant $1,000. Second and third place finishers are awarded $200 apiece.

KERRY GETZ

Philadelphia's Kerry Getz is one of the world's top street skaters, thanks to 14 years of practice and four years on the pro circuit. In 2001, among his other accomplishments, Getz snagged a street gold medal and a best-trick silver medal at the X Games in Philadelphia. ESPN ranked him as the nation's top skateboarder in 2000 when he was 25. Getz remains so obsessed with the sport that he has to order a new pair of sneakers and a new board every four or five days because they take such a beating.

Mathias Ringston soars high in the air in the skateboarding competition during the 2000 X Games in San Francisco, California.

The Games

Won some local skate competitions and think you're hot stuff? Try facing off against the masters of skateboarding in front of thousands of fans.

At two of the biggest extreme sports competitions in the world, the X Games and the Gravity Games, top skateboarders come together for a few days to showcase new tricks and compete to see who's king of the ramp.

Andy MacDonald wipes out in the skateboarding competition during the 2000 X Games in San Francisco, California.

THE GRAVITY GAMES

One of the two biggest and best-known skateboarding competitions, this nine-day celebration of extreme sports showcases seven different disciplines, all of which involve the need for speed. More than 250 athletes from almost 20 countries compete against one another in sports including skateboarding, downhill skateboarding, in-line skating, biking, freestyle motocross, street luge, and wakeboarding.

The street skateboarding competition involves no set routine. Riders use various rails, boxes, and quarterpipes to show off their stuff, with creativity being the most important element of the games. In vert competition, skaters scale 13-foot-tall (4 m), 60-inch-wide (1½ m), U-shaped halfpipes, and tear it up as much as they can within a 45-second session.

THE X GAMES

ESPN's Super Bowl of extreme sports is the best-known skateboarding competition. It's nonstop chaos and can be nonstop fun. The event's greatest highlight to date was in 1999, when Tony Hawk crossed that epic frontier of skateboarding: the 900, a midair 360-degree spin done two-and-a-half times.

X CATEGORIES

PARK: What would usually be called Street, the X Games' "Park" category consists of 20 skaters that each take two runs. Six different judges award them 0 to 100 points for the two runs combined. When they've finished their tricks and the numbers are all in, the highest and lowest numbers are dropped, the remaining four are averaged, and the skater with the highest average wins.

BEST VERT TRICK: It's a 20-minute open jam session, with judges watching until the head judge announces the session has ended.

VERT DOUBLES: Skaters pick their partners and make two runs, with the higher score used. They skate simultaneously, sometimes using each other as props. Judges in this category look mostly for originality, creativity, difficulty, and the combination of tricks.

XCELLENT LUGING: At the X Games, the two street luge events are called Super Mass and Dual. In Super Mass, groups of six competitors ride on ten-foot boards, made of aircraft-grade metals and skateboard wheels, down a twisting course at speeds of more than 60 mph (97 kph). The top three teams qualify for the next round until the final six lugers race for the podium. Dual is simply head-to-head competition in a single-elimination format.

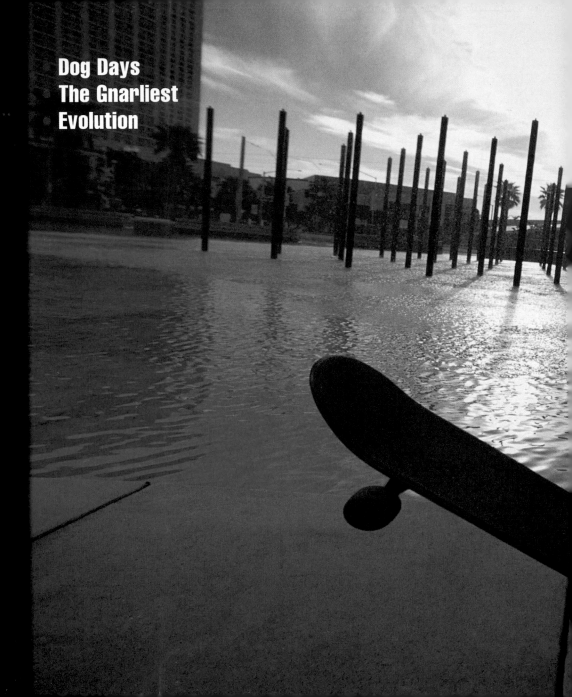

Extreme
Sports
∙∙∙∙∙∙∙∙∙∙∙∙∙∙
Part 5

Dog Days
The Gnarliest
Evolution

The Legends

Skateboarding's come a long way since the first roller-skate wheels were attached to a wood plank. Find out what it takes to go down in skate history.

Dog Days

Skateboarding was once the domain of punks who were loud, proud, and antiestablishment.

       he distinctive spirit of skateboarding took shape in the mid-1970s, when the boys of Dogtown, also know as the Z-Boys, started skateboarding in ways that no one had seen before: performing handstands, surfing empty swimming pools, and even zanier stuff.

Tony Alva skateboards in a pool in 1995.

DOGTOWN

According to most accounts, Dogtown is where skateboarding really became big. The unofficial name of the area between Santa Monica and Venice, two cities in Los Angeles, Dogtown was home to a dozen young surfers who discovered how to apply their surfing techniques to some schoolyard skate spots. The local Dogtown kids often rode low to the ground with their arms outstretched for balance, and they often skated so hard that they destroyed their homemade boards in a single session. (Back in the early 1970s, not many companies were making skateboards, so a lot of people pieced together their own equipment.)

Z-BOYS

TONY ALVA: The World Pro Champion of skateboarding in 1977, Tony Alva was one of skateboarding's great pioneers. A member of the Dogtown gang, Alva and his buddies introduced an aggressive approach to skating no one had ever seen before. Today, he has his own line of skateboards and vows he'll never quit skating.

STACY PERALTA: Stacy Peralta, another original Dogtown member, helped pioneer vert skating. He eventually left the sport to become co-owner of one of the biggest skateboarding companies in the world, Powell-Peralta, where he produced "The Bones Brigade," the first modern skateboard video, featuring top skaters sponsored by the company, including Steve Caballero, Adrian Demain, Todd Hastings, Tony Hawk, Rodney Mullen, Lance Mountain, Tommy Guerrero, and Rudy Johnson. Today, Peralta continues to produce films.

A poster for Powell-Peralta's "The Bones Brigade," the first modern skateboard video.

The Gnarliest

There are some pro skaters that manage to become more visible to fans by being gutsier, louder, and just plain better than their peers.

Tony Hawk rides the halfpipe during the Tony Hawk Skate Tour at Skater Island in Middletown, Rhode Island.

Tony Hawk is one of professional skateboarding's living legends. Kareem Campbell and Jen O'Brien are two of the sport's rising stars.

TONY HAWK

Few skaters are exceptional at both vert skating and street skating, but Tony Hawk is one. Then again, Tony Hawk seems capable of almost anything. When he was just 12 years old, for example, Hawk, born in Del Mar, California, was sponsored by Dogtown Skateboards. By age 14 he had gone pro, and by 16 he was unbeatable as the world's best skateboarder. Since then, Hawk has been in more than a hundred pro contests, three-quarters of which he has won.

Hawk only skates competitively on rare occasions these days, like at last summer's X Games, where he scored his umpteenth gold medal. But he still does several public demos a year and was recently voted the best vert skater by *Transworld Skateboarding* readers.

TONY HAWK SPECIALS

Hawk's most famous move is the 900: two-and-a-half spins in the air, first completed at the X Games in 1999. He's been creating maneuvers since 1980, though. Check out a few:

1980: Backside varial
1981: Fakie to frontside rock
1982: Gymnast plant
1983: Lipslide revert
1984: Madonna
1998: Stale fish 720
2000: 360 ollie to backside boardslide
2001: Shove-it to backside smith

KAREEM CAMPBELL

Kareem Campbell is talked about in skateboarding circles as one of the nicest athletes in the business. He's also one of the most versatile, having skated pro vert for years successfully before turning to street skating, a category in which he has become a superstar all over again. A 27-year-old father, Campbell (his friends call him "Reemo") is renowned for being ambitious. Already, he owns multiple companies, including a team called City Stars and a footwear outfit called Axion.

JEN O'BRIEN

Jen O'Brien, 24, is a top pro skateboarder who has jaw-dropping vert moves and is helping to turn what is largely a men's event professionally into one that recognizes the number of women that deserve equal footing. Not that O'Brien has anything against men who skateboard. In fact, she is married to top vert skater Bob Burnquist, and reportedly the two of them skate together in their own backyard ramp. O'Brien, alongside other female skate pros like Candy Hiler and Patty Segovia, participate each year in an event called the All-Girl Skate Jam.

Evolution

*From subculture
to mainstream,
skateboarding has kept
its integrity intact.*

While the skating world is far different from that of the early 1900s, or even the 1970s, little of the sport's fundamentals have changed. It's still all about a kid with a board having a good time challenging the limits of gravity, speed, balance, and friction.

KEEPING IT REAL

Today skateboarding has gone mainstream, and while that bothers some, most skateboarders shrug off criticism that the sport's increasing popularity is problematic. Instead, they appreciate that they can make a living doing what they love most: sick trick combos on rails, ledges, gaps, ramps—or wherever their boards will go.

FULL CIRCLE

Skateboarding's focus has also shifted over the years. Starting with horizontal moves, freestyle and slalom skateboarding dominated until skateboarders starting going vertical in the mid-1970s. Top riders included Tony Alva, Jay Adams, and Tom "Wally" Inouye. Toward the end of the 1980s, skateboarding shifted focus again, from vert skating, which became less popular, to street skating, which concentrated more on technical tricks. Meanwhile, some pro skaters decided to start their own skate companies.

Today, street skating is as popular as ever, longboarding is back, and downhill skateboarding has entered a new dimension, thanks to the daring sport of street luge.

GOING OLD SCHOOL

Going old school means borrowing the best from the past and making it work for you in today's world. Some skaters like the history or nostalgic aspect of using boards and trucks that are no longer available. Others just like the fact that it's different. Old-school skateboards are usually boards that were produced in the 1980s or earlier that have, for some reason, come and gone. To find them, you typically have to negotiate with a private collector or try bidding for one online at an auction site.

Skate Smarts

- **Rules for the Rugged**
- **Shape Up**

Confidence, guts, and even a bit of attitude are assets to any skateboarder. But ride smart, or you won't be riding for long.

Rules for the Rugged

Skateboarding is an extreme sport, but if you follow the rules and use common sense, you'll have a good time—without getting hurt.

Ride with awareness and respect—especially when it comes to the public and law enforcement. You'll be doing yourself, and the sport as a whole, a great service.

Brian Howard slides down the ramp after he falls during the vert event at the 2001 X Games in San Diego, California.

SKATING RULES

1. Skate with your crew. It's more fun, and if someone has a nasty spill, you can go for help—or vice versa.

2. Always wear a helmet, elbow pads, and knee pads, with special emphasis on the helmet (see sidebar). Not all skateparks require them, but why risk cracking your noggin when you plan to have a long life ahead of you?

3. If you're riding after sunset, wear reflective clothing.

4. If it's snowing, don't even think about it. Not only do you risk freezing your hand to your skateboard's trucks—it happens!—but your bearings won't roll well, your deck has a better chance of snapping, and the pain of falling when it's cold out is far worse than when it's not. Furthermore, having to wear layers of clothing to stay warm will restrict your movement.

5. Never ride (or do a trick) above your level. It's great to challenge yourself (and that's part of the fun), but if you don't think you're ready for a tough trick, don't attempt it. There's a not-so-fine line between being gutsy and being dumb.

DON'T LEAVE HOME WITHOUT 'EM

HELMET: Get one that fits your melon snugly, and wear it at all times.

KNEE PADS: The pros wear them. You should, too.

SKATE SHOES: A pair with an air-cushioning unit and a gum-rubber outsole for traction is the way to go.

WATER BOTTLES: Have them around. You're going to be sweating plenty, and you need to replenish what you lose.

GRIP TAPE: It's what keeps you from slipping off your board. You can get it with graphics, and it's easily replaceable at just $6 a sheet.

GLOVES: Get special plastic-sided ones for sliding from your nearest skateboard retailer or online.

Shape Up

Everything hinges on you and your board, so keep both in good shape.

I t might cut into your skateboarding schedule, but to make your board last, a weekly checkup is a good idea, starting with a long, hard look at your bearings.

SKATEBOARD MAINTENANCE

BEARINGS Cleaning them is a piece of cake. It requires paint thinner, a couple of paper towels, and usually some bearing lubricant like WD-40. Just unscrew the axle nut while holding onto your wheel, and take the wheel off. Dab the paper towel in paint thinner, and use it to wipe clean the dirt and other gunk on the bearing's outside. Then stuff the thinner-soaked towel into the opening in the truck where the wheel goes, twist it around, and clean that out, too. Finally, before screwing the axle nut back on, apply a touch of bearing lubricant to it.

TRUCKS Trucks can come unhinged, so spend a few minutes tightening your hardware on occasion. It's far less irritating than spending months nursing a broken arm because your trucks fell off when you dropped onto concrete from some mammoth height.

DECKS All decks eventually wear out. Cracks are a killer, but you can save your deck if it's just starting to chip by using carpenter's glue as a sealant. Also, keep in mind that even the best companies sometimes make defective decks, so if yours starts coming apart sooner than seems normal, take it back.

SKATEBOARDER MAINTENANCE

Skateboarding will make your heart race faster, your legs more muscle-bound, and your mind more clear. Still, when you're not on your board, consider a few outside activities, like running, surfing, or skiing, that can enrich your life, your health, and your skateboarding.

Increasing your endurance and muscle tone is the idea. Other important ways to stay on top of your game: Learn where your center of gravity is, and know which way is up when you're spinning in the air. Practice focusing on something immovable when you're in motion that can give you some sense of where you are.

OTHER TRAINING TIPS

WATCH YOUR DIET. They say you are what you eat. Knowing that, would you rather look and feel like a greasy cheeseburger or a lean, mean fighting machine, which is what eating complex carbohydrates, like vegetables and fresh fruit, will help you become?

DRINK WATER. A lot of it. You should normally drink around eight glasses of H_2O each day. You'll need more if you're skating hard.

SKATEBOARD ALL THE TIME. You probably don't need any incentive to get out on your board daily. But the unavoidable, and not unattractive, truth is that if you want to get good you should be skating constantly. In fact, many of the pros log upwards of eight hours each day. (Unless you're planning to make skateboarding your life's work, that's probably a little much. But you get the idea.)

Resources

ADDITIONAL INFORMATION ON SKATEBOARDING

WEB SITES

Here are some Web sites you can check out to find general information on skateboarding, skatepark locations, and skateboard events.

Big Brother (magazine): www.bigbrothermagazine.com

Jimmy Eat World: www.jimmyeatworld.net

Skateboard Directory: www.skateboarddirectory.com

Skateboarder (magazine): www.skateboardermag.com

Skateboarding Association of America: skateboardassn.org

Skatepark Association of the United States of America: www.spausa.org

Transworld Skateboarding (magazine): www.skateboarding.com

The Ultimate Skateboard Park Directory: www.skateboardParks.com

Thrasher (magazine): www.thrashermagazine.com

Tony Hawk: www.tonyhawk.com

United Skateboard Association: www.unitedskate.com

Vans Warped Tour: warpedtour.launch.com

World Freestyle Skateboard Association: www.reversefreestyle.com/wfsa

Z-Boys: www.z-boys.com

SKATE CAMPS

Lake Owen: Lake Owen, Wisconsin

SDG Skatepark Camp: Tempe, Arizona

Skater Island: Middletown, Rhode Island

Woodward Camp: Woodward, Pennsylvania

ABOUT THE AUTHOR

Constance Loizos is a San Francisco-based writer who fondly remembers her first skateboard, a canary yellow number with transparent white wheels. She has written for a variety of publications, including *Business Week, Inc., Fast Company,* and *Sport.*

ACKNOWLEDGEMENTS

Special thanks to Andrew Piper, Mike Freemantle, and Soren Roth.

PHOTO CREDITS

Ezea Shaw/AllSport: Pages 2, 44, 46; AllSport: Pages 4, 20, 21, 30, 34, 38, 39, 62, 63; Corbis Royalty Free: Pages 6, 10, 11, 12, 14, 18, 19, 22, 50, 56, 57, 58, 61; PhotoDisc: Pages 8, 16, 23, 26, 45, 49, 53 left; Comstock: Page 13; Tom Hauck/AllSport: Pages 24, 37, 60; Corel: Pages 25, 35; David Leeds/AllSport: Pages 28, 48; Photos Courtesy of Mike Freemantle: Page 31; Simon Bruty/AllSport: Page 32; Harry How/AllSport: Page 36; Scott Starr: Page 40; John Ferrey/AllSport: Page 42; Jed Jacobsohn/AllSport: Page 47; Tina Schmidt/AllSport: Page 52; SkateOne: Page 53 right; Jamie Squire/AllSport: Page 54; Patty Segovia/Silver Photo Agency: Page 24, 55

Library of Congress Cataloging-in-Publication Data Available Upon Request

ISBN: 0-7922-8229-9

Design and Editorial: Bill SMITH STUDIO Inc.
Series design: Joy Masoff